OYSTER

OYSTER

Michael Pedersen

with illustrations by
Scott Hutchison

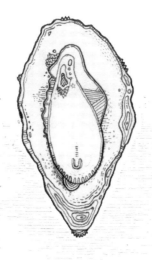

Polygon

This edition first published in
Great Britain in 2017 by Polygon,
an imprint of Birlinn Limited
West Newington House, 10 Newington Road
Edinburgh, EH9 1QS

9 8 7 6 5 4

www.polygonbooks.co.uk

Print ISBN: 978 1 84697 397 0
eBook ISBN: 978 0 85790 935 0

British Library Cataloguing-in-Publication Data
A catalogue record for this book is available from the
British Library.

Typeset in Verdigris MVB by Polygon
Printed and bound by TJ International, Padstow, Cornwall

CONTENTS

Obsessive Cannibal Love Poem*   1

Starry-Eyed*   2

Kung Fu Fighting   5

Gravity*   6

Cannae Sleep*   8

Highland Koo*   11

Big Feardie   14

Swallow the Pill   16

Limelite Bar, Meadowbank   18

Fancy Dress for Fancy Folks*   20

Oyster*   23

Middle November, Paris, 2015   26

What was Supposed to be an Angry One   31

When you Came to me in Grez-sur-Loing*   32

Birds & Trains   34

Ying-Yang-Wrang-Wan-Right   37

When they got together they knew
    what they weren't   38

Antipodeans   41

Cliff & Noc   42

Rollercoasters   45

Finding Grace   47

James Dovetail   51

life of owen   53

I'm a PC   56

Invitation for Luncheon with Caddy D 58

John Up High 62

Birthday BBQ, 2008 64

Manchester John: Episode II 66

Christmas at Omega Sauna 68

WI 71

WI(III) 73

When Carla Moved Out 75

Hey Ho Here Comes Colin 77

Transmorphisizing* 79

Greetin' fur Gretna Green 81

Humping Cows 84

FUCK! 86

A Year, Aye? 90

Totem Pole Capable 91

Conversation Overheard in Craigmillar
  Dental Practice 93

R v Brown 96

Free Personality Test, Sir?! 98

Superstition & Superheroes 100

(In between) Mud & Stars 103

Portree's Lost & Found 105

Guide to Space Proofing your Robot Heart 109

Deep, deep down* 113

Hello, I am Scotland* 114

Acknowledgements 117

*Audio recordings of these poems are available from the publisher, see page 120 for more information.

Dedication

Lush love to you, who has opened this book. This is the fourth edition of our curious *Oyster*. So thank you, all you oyster eaters, thanks fondly and fervently wi aw them gooey bits. May its salty smooch spill doon yer chin.

To launch this oddball out into the world, my best friend Scott John Hutchison (H-Craft) and I unshackled a UK tour that catapulted us to a run of shows in South Africa, including a stunning exhibition of Scott's illustrations. Though Scott and I had been close chums for years, these shows, and our time together, was yin of the best, the most enriching, vibrant, loved and enthralling periods of my life. This book is not a collaboration but a muckle monument to a friendship that flew.

The shows together must stop, we lost Scott in May 2018. But H-Craft, this book is yours and to you always – you brilliant, beautiful human.

A best to many I've no doubt, rightly and most righteously so. You are gone now (as we know it) and that is not, nor will it ever be okay. The formidable and abundant void you left spills among us, it encases us like wax, like arms, like the ocean. This same force shall unify us, for in it is the befuddling beauty of an entire galaxy of magnets – it is your pull, you supreme magnet, you clever bearded bastard, glimmering moon of a man.

Let's keep talking, awiz – uh luv ye.

(x)(x)

Obsessive Cannibal Love Poem

Today is *yes please* and *now* to zipping your
skin around me, to wrapping up in you
like a winter coat with matching scarf
and walking barefoot on powdered snow,
you: the flakes squeezing
between my toes; the biscuits I brought
to snack on are your bones baked
and sweetened; like counting stars
I do not think I will ever be done
kissing you: honey all over
and deep inside, I will swallow
your dancing tongue; take your
daydreams into my nightdreams, all
neu-wave heavenly, ethereal gleam
on wet tarmac, enemy of the rain
which fell between us, which has
no business being there.

Other days a text message
or quick chat on the phone
will do just fine –
I never can tell.

Starry-Eyed

There are scientists with mouths
agape, eyes gazing
at Saturn's rings: a satellite's sink
and swing make it so, unveil
space secrets, star trails, objects
born of light and dust.
If a bell rings in space
they'll have an idea how it
sounds, they probably put it
there: can a bell ring underwater?
you're maybe thinking – me
too. Not a bell but a crash
in the rings has caught their eye,
a swell of disturbance created
by a creature: Peggy.
At the time of writing, reader,
Peggy has never exposed herself:
what's seen is the ripples
pulsing, ripples rising. We
know what she's not: not
a moonlet, which would part
the dust more violently – so
a non-moonlet – not biblical, not
a fish, the ripples are not akin
to those on Scottish lochs. Peggy
leaves a hole in the rings like

an antique brooch needling
into a cashmere scarf
– the gaps in the rings will
reform and bauble yet always
be different; not the same
as water, helixed and twisted
through propeller blades
which remains water, but
not so different either.

They're hunting Peggy's ghost,
slug tracks, mouse droppings.
Don on the job,
satellite-wise, is Cassini.
Leering and loitering best and longest,
after years of Peggy
shadow-stalking, Cassini's
reign on Saturn's lip
is trembling to a close. Retirement,
sure, but Cassini will not
come home, instead will capture
one last supreme
and crowning image of Peggy.
One last before plunging into
the fast flying debris. One last before
eternal destruction.
A martyr to the moves of Peggy,
perhaps touching the same

dust, perhaps, in the future,
being part of a dustbin elbowed
out the way as Peggy
rushes by, a snowy smear
of glowy smudge, penumbra
winking down, and grinning
through the nebulae.

Scientists will call the end
of Cassini a migration.
Mission complete,
they'll clink Champagne
and plot another probe.
The end of Cassini
will be a 75,000
mile-an-hour collision,
a jet propulsion watched
from an earthly laboratory.
Cassini will get a moment
of silence before the drinking
starts; Cassini is carrying
the question of life,
Cassini is a genius
in just one word, not
just a scientific success
but an act of desperation:
requited and unrequited love.
Cassini has left
the space business.

Kung Fu Fighting

I should like to karate kick
all your insecurities
square
on
the chin
(KIAI!):
perfect force
and
flawless precision;
a trained, toned,
muscular limb.
To date, I've just
been shoving at 'em,
pub brawling,
odd prod
in the ribs or
jab tae the chest.
If I finished
the job, sparkled
'em, if your world
stopped wavering
because of them,
would you still need
my arms and legs –
you'd be so
strong yourself?

Gravity

I love you,
she said, as if wearing someone
else's skin,
as if clocking in
then out
of the nine-to-five
that tired her bones.
I love you, she said
with the forced verve of waves
gargling oily pebbles from
a spill, its fringe, a congealing shoreline: talk
laced with salt, a tongue
socked in sand. *I love you,*
she said, with the mechanical bareness
of a warden clamping a car
to the pavement,
the payment meter and itself;
choking on diesel that once
made an engine purr; a majestic gull sifting
through a city's birthing gunk, cum,
love's tragic overspill.
I love,
she said.
I love
you,

with the frankness of caffeinated truths
in the morning after our own golden Armageddon
which is as welcome as Nirvana.
I love you, half price,
with the candour of when we never really knew each other,
bridal curiosity ringing, rings setting up the eyes.
I love you,
in a way
we never touch upon in joviality;
in a way
we never rediscovered that raw sexuality;
in a way
we have time to tread
water – that's no good thing.

I love you, with saccharine warmth
for our own self-pleasantries.
With everything we're floating.
We promised to make things float.
Were we not supposed to (this once made us) F L O A T?

Cannae Sleep

If not for that blasted boiler bellowing
as if hawking up soot and phlegm
or a nettling sensation parading
over freckled skin; if not for
your legs jolting like a wind-up
toy gone bananas or the fact I
hear breath, feel and nearly see
breath at the foot of the bed; if not for
roving creatures smearing
handprints over the damp,
rattling window on which
the moon has painted itself,
I'd be sound asleep, blissfully dreaming,
sculpting plots so gratifying
I'd applaud myself on waking,
remarking, *well dreamt kid*,
in the manner of a baseball coach
praising an underrated player,
whose homer just won the game.

If not for shattered bone
tightening in my right index,
triggering a seeping pain
which sluggishly curls
around breaks that never quite
healed; if not for that second

cup of heaped coffee, abundant
sugar in wine; if not for rock
shock wilderness challenging
far-off vastness, if not for
a lack of mental shelf space
or the storm outside shaking the air
like tambourines, rainsticks and maracas,
the wind, full cantata, torpedoing
trees, howling like an orgy
of giddy banshees, terrifying
the neighbour's darling
kids; or the thought of
missing cats drenched 'n' greetin'
sheltering in doorways,
the meat on them attracting
Thought Foxes, the cinematic
plop of weighty drips plus the clock:
that fucking clock, tick-tocking
though the hands fell off
years ago; if not for unlit
candles wobbling on china
saucers keen to burn –
implying they could be smoking stars – illuminating
the scuffed boots and cracked pots below; if not
for shapes and figures
swirling around in darkness
like paint splat on water for marbling
paper; if not for my scant body hair

making itself known, gloating
and breeding, if not
for aw o' that, I'd be sound, sound
asleep; all of that and today's late
rise and the poker-faced
clerk in Tesco that got me
thinking: *I've lost many more*
morals than I'd care to admit. Yes, all, all,
all of that and one last
secret (or two) I daren't even utter
or you'd wake up, sit
bolt upright and that'd be
the end of that.

Highland Koo

              you are massive
and ginger, no effulgent like Irn-Bru
but light and sandy, pollens and rust.

King o' Celts, lionized as thistles and
oor Rabbie – yer puss ower postcards,
tea towels and them rubbishy tins.

Yid dae fine in London or America,
alien of extraordinary ability, but
those hooves wouldnae trot

anywhere else. Koo, yer horns
are like Triassic tusks atop yer heid,
reckon you could square-go a tiger

if bullied intae it, put Desperate Dan
on his erse – nae bother; but you're no bam
Koo, naw, starting nuthin wi nae one,

fringe over yer een, bonfire in thon
belly; sure, you play it cool, scoff
grass, scart yerself rotten on fences,

power through the shitey weather,
take a plunge in the modest sun;
drink it in, as yiv a'ways done

KOO.

Big Feardie

Ah think ah seen this car coming, right,
zipping through Windsor Street like
a rusty apparition, it's bat-black dark
oot, pure baltic, honds in ma pockets,
the sky riled is belting doon upon us.
I'm weaving through the sharp sleek air
bobbing ma heid as if dodging bullets
in the rain, as if in a wartime air raid,
my coupon key artillery. This car:
nae lights oan, ah cin barely spy it at first
but then this lassie sparks up a fag and
shape casts itself: side-panels, bonnet,
roof aw appear, sudden as if oot
from under an invisible cloak. See
ah thinks to signal wi those flashing 'hings
where you try to chuck aw ten fingers
off yer honds; cause ah ken she's copped us
wi nae idea she's night rider incarnate
but then, as ah say, it's blue baws freezing
and likely another good Samaritan,
wi gloves oan, will save the day
or the daftie will suddenly git it.
So paws stay in pockets as she speeds on by
an' ah zone back into ma tunes
but there's nae solace, moral dilemma
spits oot wi a vengeance: ah hear

a screeching 'n' a screaming; look
ower ma shoulder but it's kicked aff
roond the corner and am a stane's
throw fae the gaff noo, so no stopping
fur naebody – she'll huv whacked intae
a wheelie bin blown ontae the road or
collided wi a double parked vehicle –
nippy likes but *sans dévastation*.
Aw'body will get over it, ah
already huv. But here's the 'hing,
I read the next day she's done
much worse, real bile up fae
the stomach and red retina
ruinous stuff, she's ploughed doon
a mother and her dug, and that's
no the end of it, the mother had a
bairn strapped tae her belly.

Now ma mitts are feeling heavy
and I take a different route,
it's nae colder, just seems so;
'n' it doesnae shift the feeling
that I've lost mair than sleep here,
that I'm mair than a tad culpable. See,
difference is, she didnae see
it coming, me, I was simply fucking
lazy; lazy and feart a' the cold.

Swallow the Pill

I come fae ma Da, aw Danish ginger
brain 'n' bristle, fair fire in 'em, I've felt
that scorch, we're fichters – fur good
and bad; him being mair auld fashioned
aboot smoking and shagging but me
kindae gettin that. I come fae ma Ma,
giddy-daft fur watching 'hings grow:
flooers, fruit 'n' veg, sun in sky, butter
-flies in oor bellies we didnae talk aboot.
I come fae Scotland – took me years tae
cheer, years and thoosands of miles – doon
Durham and Nottingham, London, Cambodia,
mair, then hame. I come fae ma Gran, wee
Jessie Lee that a'wis caws herself stupit, who's
roseate smile and humble biscuit face is
any'hing but – aye, she got tricked into
voting UKIP by a wily gadgie that chapped
her door, but we'll get him guid. I come
fae aw them books I've read, no the ones
ah pretended tae when trying no tae lose
face at Law School. I come fae losing
face, then getting ower it, fae heartbreak
and battling failed romances wi peev
and drugs; I come fae been a lawyer
doon sooth, then even better, chucking
it in, come fae that smug Eton cunt

caw'in me Jock and Smelly Sock,
in a board meeting, then asking if I was
from the Gorbals. I come fae no
smacking him around the coupon wi ma
cock afore answering meekly, naw,
that's in Glasgow. Fuck me, I'm coming
UP in a big way and, warl',
I'm comin fur you.

Limelite Bar, Meadowbank

She comes at me quickly, wasp-like, lips twitching, pulsing
and eyes frantic: *Ehhhh . . . I need a fucking word wi you.*

Uh-huh, what's this all about then? I'm retorting calmly
bringing balance to messy panic; her face is sweating,

my palms are too. *I heard YOU called ma da a Nazi!* –
foaming at the mooth, shoving imaginary strangers, summoning

her inner bully – a fond pastime. Me, I'm in a pickle:
this chimes true, I've said it several times: *Erm, well . . .* [fuck

it] . . . *aye, I did.* The scene shifts – screaming starts – gaping fury:
Boaaaaab! Boab! [summoning thon partner] *He's no even denying it!*

Now cushioned behind her, Boab looms in, formidable and solid.
He fucking well called ma da a Nazi. Fuck d'ya think yer playing

at? Boab is unquestionably present but *not quite* ready to pounce,
so ah take a shot, exhale, legal reasoning: *Well, he does collect Nazi*

memorabilia, though labeling this a hobby fuelled by historical
interest, he too, has flung a Hitler salute this way chanting Sieg Heil

with his cadre as a means of intimidation – a ceremonial snarl at
a well-kent liberal belief system; season into that a previous upset

involving your da and his brother attempting to sign me up to UKIP –
a party whose ideals they applaud, yet I abhor – and we

have a strong case. She takes a moment, digests. *Aye well, he could get in*
a lot 'a fucking trouble, he works fur the Scottish Exec, Social Policy

Department, ya ken that. I know, I respond coolly, then continue:
Look at it this way, if he was that upset he'd have deleted me

as friend on Facebook, naw? Boab agrees, the matter is closed.
The couple depart bickering as a champion's swig is taken.

Fancy Dress for Fancy Folks

We, us pair, in beautiful wigs, shimmy
through the busy streets, our moon faces
full like Christmas bellies. Our coy,
coiling grins greet friends and
strangers': *hullllllooh and-very-berry-*
merry-nice-and-soon-YES-yes; we get home,
exhausted, unclip our smiles, they fall
to the floor with the heavy thud
of metal chains and evening wraps us. Rapt
in its heft we're a new fur coat; we let our wigs
slip from our scalps, peel open in undress,
think the first peek of banana between skin
– looks right rough you'd think, what's
underneath, until you touched it, treat
it to a cheek rub. Such secrets we keep.
Nearly naked, all our little aerials ready
to receive: the body, its treacle, its gloss.
Mission control: they need not be bright
as beach life, just need a good scour
of sand, sea, salt and sun. Fix your
bones to mine, become a coital bow,
it is Christmas Eve and us in wigs and high
heels, clogs, frocks and frowns are now
in none; public, are now private.
So come, let us strip together, forever,

eat snow, warn each other to enjoy it for
this hot fleshy love, in the bigger
picture, holds us only for seconds,
a snowflake on the tongue.

Oyster

Bums to seats down at the table –
in every direction universes beyond this
room glimmer and creak, skies
strain, though I do not notice,
my eyes are lit like candles:
chatter swoops and whispered words
whisk up a clamour, the clink
of glasses rustle bread in baskets.
She licks wined lips and then
my oyster: *sluuuuuuup*, kissing
me, kissing sea. A lifelong
veggie: *une mère, une femme,*
une runaway bandit – her pink propulsive
tongue a creature of its own.
No bones in tongue nor oyster,
though a marvel nonetheless:
a zinc-pumped seabed filter system,
oyster has many magics and molluscy
mischief, is worthily lickable –
yet she had never licked an oyster!
Her tongue recoils gingerly, processing
them flavoursome fecundities;
the fleshy grope is silent and wordless,
the moment's *après*, noisy and weird,
rattle around, shake out a timid smile.
Not to be bested, the oyster too tastes

tongue, zaps back, a shiver to the spine
from the aquatic journeyman.
How does tongue taste to oyster?
Best not to know.

This meeting, six months back, was
its own never-never land, a hunk of
'would never happen, nae hope in hell' –
yet here we are plucky as moon
still out in morning, sat thigether
in Paris's Latin Quarter, watching,
wi the een of plotting seagulls,
this salt-laced mystery-trip unravel.
I'm staring down both barrels at
your stars, born out of sparks:
you licked my oyster, you are
the oyster licker, one brilliantly bizarre
little alien meets another for pearlescent
new discovery. Clink the glass, for
the very oyster you licked
echoes down my throat now – the mischief
in your mollusc my tongue
understands. [1]

---

1. *Optional ruminative sentiment:*
A word of advice, if licking an oyster
for your first and perhaps only time,
make sure it's by candlelight:
long wicks to cast shadow
on old wood, the type of shadow
whose bodiless limbo might just stick
around; maybe one year
and three months on, the same
tongue will farm your
cappuccino foam, unearth
an, all over, elation.

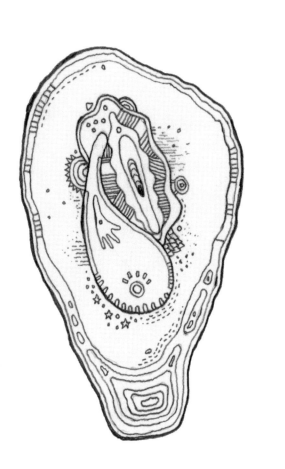

Middle November, Paris, 2015

(i)

It was the eleventh, a train
fae Bourron-Marlotte-Grez
to Gare de Lyon, 3.2 miles
across Paris to Rue de Berri,
to BBC's French HQ. It wis *moi*,
beamed by radio back to you
Caledonia tae talk residencies,
read words by Robert Louis
Stevenson, wish him *aw the best*
for an impending birthday, his 165th,
in two days time.
It wis Red

Wednesday, Remembrance
Day, streets
thronged wi beautiful people fancifully
clad, fanciest folk filtered into
Le Palais de l'Élysée where French
flags clustered thigether in bouquets,
ubiquity mirrored *only* by the
uniformed police, their firepower,

road-blocks. *What's the mood in Paris?*
Janice asked; I've edged forwards
to shuffle oot the question,
castigating myself utterly useless
at this foreign correspondent stuff,
too caught up in buildings and
shadow. We giggle wi insouciance,
move on. I really wanted
to say I felt rich as brandy butter but
a little lonely, hud
asked Paris to 'hold me like
you've never held another lover'
– was awaiting the response.

(ii)

That night, re-arriving in Grez, aw
public transport ceased, town's
only taxi 'taking a month off'; and thick
stilling darkness scarfed around the forest.
Hud to walk two miles
down the flank of a motorway
to get back to Hotel Chevillon – headlights
glaring, fog encasing, horns
and engines snarling every step
o' the way; it was my heart and feet
that took the pummeling.

(iii)

It was Friday, 21.58, in grassy
outskirts, I sent an email to Bréon
imploring a snappy visit –
hurry along chum, soon the wind
whisks John Giorno in, his New York
sass at Palais de Tokyo, let's share
that, wash him down with Beaujolais
Nouveau – what a rich buffet of
flavours to taste, old friend.

22.10 and I got word
of the City under siege, stayed-up
wi the night letting friends know I was safe,
feeling stupid about that, jumping
between news channels hosting
all sorts of poppycock, shrinking
every time the death count rose.
Next day I walked in tune
with sunset, ragged silhouettes
of plump trees that spilled themselves
were laced in and corseted
by dark. It was a fine inky
night but I didn't dare look
anything in the eye: not
chubby trees, not lamp posts,
mailboxes; most of all, not persons.

For a minute, it was honeyed
reverie ahead of your arrival,
aw sex and kissing and river
walking, hand-holding, quixotic
promises holding nu'hing
of atrocity. Reader,
this reverie broke free,
I snapped swift-like fingers
from the guilt of it.

(iv)

Cornering Rue Wilson is Rue Renoult,
down there is more rural still;
pass rue-to-rue-to-rue, thinking, *fuck
if I can't daydream of lust and love,
aw might as well end now . . .*
so ah stopped, astounded,
confronted: it was a lad of fifteen
or so, on aw fours, putting finishing
touches on the most elaborate
Christmas display spied
for silly years, must have
been ages at it, laying foundations,
rigging power supplies,
sculpting figures: igloos,
penguins, snowmen, Santa on
a swing, Santa on a sleigh,

Santa scampering up the roof;
carpeting the scene with faux
snow, chintzy lights and a big
bastard tree, towering like
the Empire State. Like any great

sculptor the boy took time
to appraise his work. Satisfied,
he traded a knowing glance,
mumbled something
indecipherable in French, voice full
of pubescent crackle. In
amongst the sermon, I heard the
words: *espoir, amour, avenir*;
nodded, as if applauding,
and hurried along. It was
what it was – not nothing.

What was Supposed to be an Angry One

You came at me in pop songs.
Gung-ho, little candyfloss killer,
an anthemic infantry, by headphone
and live wire: YES I'm listening now.
Roused, I feel you now, running
the world: zipping up, heading out,
cherry bombs in duffle pocket, a
Chinese Rocket brooding behind
toggled buttons – take it all, from
Sauchiehall to the Brill Building.

I think of you in stillness *en Grez-sur*
-Loing, washing in the nippy river – nippy,
it's fucking freezing, chills dig
bone-deep, nettling cheeks
watermelon red; fast as you splash
the stream sets quicker, reshapes,
reflects: eyes, hair, Scottishness, sky – a
reformation within ripples; what
I'd hope for. I hurt you more (your
songs, they say so), I'm sorry. I am
sorry. An offering: one circle, bent out of shape,
doesn't roll so blithely
down the hill. But look closely, aw
mangled, that square you mentioned,
scratched and bashed, off kilter,
might noo fit through.

When you Came to me in Grez-sur-Loing

We never rode the boat downstream –
ah couldnae even find it, never
hud them bicycles oot, filled
their baskets or skinny dipped
in the gelid river. I took you walking
doon a motorway, only restaurant
in toon wis shut, wis also the bar,
nightlife tae boot. Our prize-winning
baker went awiy on *sojourn*
day of yer arrival and I'd been
sending teasing snaps of his
baguettes and sugared tarts –
that wee French fancy, never hud
a crumb o' it. The shower blocked.
It overflowed, you stood in shit
in Nemours. Thon mansion hoose
festooned in Festive décor,
garish as yiv ever seen,
yi never saw; it rained, poured, air
frosted, nipped like a bairn's
pinch, that puckish kid ah wis warring
wi never showed his ruddy face.
Petite merde, we never fucked
in the forest in those tube socks
I canonised, there's a cum stain
on your new silk dress, I fell asleep

on the final night though you were
feeling chatty: aw that happened and
never happened when yi came
for me in Grez-sur-Loing.
But let me tell you this, you made
the wind seem safter, the giant
auburn leaves glaw, the tumbling
stream turned susurrus, so more
birdsong, ah know. We kissed
for oors and it felt like hardly
gettin' started, wiz great, your
hands, your tongue, the way
they run, wiz great; and I'm pretty
sure we fell in love some. Love begins
to balance 'hings oot, or near
enough for noo; and though the
baker and the restaurateur re-opened
wi sly scheming unison, and town's
lights beamed oot as aw
sung carols o' joy and grace,
it was never better, never, *not ever*,
than you, here, in their place.

Birds & Trains

Today in Paris, you are sticky
tongued, whistle wet – of buzzards
thermalling above the Campsies,
whose wings disrupt a rainbow,
we do not have the foggiest. So memory
don't bowdlerise the technicolour
of today's deep bath, champagne
flutes full as expectation. Steaming,
we are hissing chestnuts, hot as fresh
soap, hot as kind eyes. Mind you,
in retrospect, Hollie prefers
the bath a little cooler. A few days
from now yer gone from here and I am
relishing a moment not a butter-soft
bare bum. It is cooler, whispering
November rain, birds are up,
hefty trains heave by and you
are in Cambridge as Paris puffs out
its chest. Birds and trains I love to
wake to, our great migrants, custodians
of perpetual movement, fucking
fascinating things – one engineered
majesty, the other . . . in fact that
goes fur both. I know little of
ornithology but there is a sense,
an arcane scale of distance

in chirruping beaks, in wheels
grinding down track. Yet Hollie, more
than the sound of singing birds
cracking open new days and trains
powering off maps, more than that,
I like to wake to pictures of you,
a comet coruscating, weaving
words by loose tongue and lovely
licks; thoughts travelling
as electricity, way too fast
to be caught by the mind
that made them. Yer ethereal
edges, clouds in carousel,
in as much as a cloud can
carousel – wherever's whenever.
These reveries are toe-tinglers,
stomach somersault-ers,
trapeze artists of the mind.
So dinnae dare apologise for filling
an inbox during the nicht
for I am alone in France still basking
in your taste, eating your aubergine
bake; and come let's take a train ride
thigether: The Blue Grain, Pride
of Africa, Palace on Wheels,
Devil's Nose, Glacier Express,
yes I looked them up and, heck,
The Flying Scotsman will do

because your lips beckon me
like birdsong to soft and slurping
swathes of juicy SMOOCH!
Greater, faster, further than before.
Like passing trains, we might not
often share the same steel shed
or carry similar cargo, but our
locomotion synced-up is something
sublime and like birds, of feathers every
colour, we make a fantastic racket.

Ying-Yang-Wrang-Wan-Right

Sometimes I think we're all wrong
for each other, inverses, salt
in coffee; other times, it's, yup, perfect
fit, tailored tight to the millimetre – I'm
breathing through you, keys of a zip
releasing in unison; this is how
we fell, fell, fell
in love.

When they got together they knew what they weren't

WOMAN: I love you.

MAN: I love you more.

WOMAN: No, I love you more.

MAN: No ME! I Love you more.

WOMAN: I – LOVE – you – more!

MAN: No, no . . . Iloveyoumore.

WOMAN: Me. It's me – loving you more!

MAN: I love you I love you I love you! More more more.

WOMAN: I LOVE YOU. I love you MORE!

MAN: No, it's me, me me. I love you more and more and more and more and more.
I LOVE YOU moremoremore moremore more more moremore moremoremore mmmmmmmmmmmmmmore

moremoremoremoremoremoremoremoremor
moremoremoremoremoremore
more MORE!

WOMAN: Hmmmmmmmmmm.

MAN: You see it now don't you – I love you more
           times infinity multiplied by aaaaaaalllllll
           the kisses I'm still to give you – the world is
           off its axis with the weight.

WOMAN: Aye, I think you're probably right.

           You've become a right soppy cunt since I
           got my coil in!

           If I'm honest, it's starting to do ma heid
           in!

MAN: . . .

Antipodeans

She had the desert glow, the blithe
gait of a girl who'd travelled Australia,
loved it. I felt an instant relief
– slipping into images of her
bodyboarding, quaffing cheap beer,
mimicking an Aussie accent,
talking about Scotland as a list
of quiz facts on a cereal box.

In photographs
she would strike handstands as her skirt
tipped down, high-five wide-
mouthed men in shirts flapping open or off;
would extend both arms up in the air
as if celebrating a goal then jump
onto somebody's back making
a whooping sound. If only
all my ex-lovers would explore
Oz, I would feel no pain.

Cliff & Noc

*Written upon the discovery of a Beluga Whale Mimicking the
Human Voice, 2012.*

I am a night-guard
at San Diego's National Marine Mammal Foundation
(NMMF); my name is Cliff.
I have four children by two different women.
I drink Budweiser, king of beers,
mostly to forget things I remember too well.
I smoke Parliament cigarettes
with a recessed charcoal filter.
I fair better at night, alone, speaking rarely.
I'm not always happy, I like it
being just me and the marine life.
I was once more man, less tired,
someone's please-sit-on-my-suitcase
-full-of-holiday-clothes-so-that-I-can
-zip-it-shut, thanked with a kiss.

Last night during my sixth cigarette
I encountered an ebullient Philip,
the Foundation's Senior Marine Biologist
He informed me
of a breakthrough, that could:
(a)   propel his career forward;
(b)   propel his career upward;

(c)   make national headlines; and

(d)   enlighten

the field. A Beluga whale named Noc
had been warbling like a human warbles,
garbling so well it tricked the lot of them.

What ensued was a jubilant burst
of detail: nasal passage flaring; inflating
air sacs; a small plastic device; pressure
levels corresponding to high vocalisations.
I, sort of, understood.
There was talk of multiplied funding,
new departments, an influx
of international visitors, researchers,
more night-guards.

Philip scurried off
leaving me perturbed, alarmed,
weakened by the thought
of such a flurry. Last month
in the heat of moment,
I had said some rude things to Noc about
the NMMF Management Team and Advisory Board:
had stolen
from the dolphin donation box and once
flicked cigarette ash
in the stingray tank.

My first thought was to smash
the device in Philip's office
but I knew I'd get caught – Philip
was very smart and I am reckless.

So, as much as I hated to, I threatened
Noc: *Whatever you have to say*
just keep it to yourself. Let me tell you,
it's the blabby ones that get caught
in propellers, iced and sliced for a seasonal meal
or opened up for oil.
Parrots have been talking for years
and it hasn't done them any good.
I'd keep quiet if you know what's good for you.

Up until this point, Noc had considered
me a friend. I felt lugubrious as a murky puddle,
ugly as a wart.

Anything else to say? I roared through tears.

Noc never replied, not ever again.

Rollercoasters

Eighteen and the cunt shot
you clean in the coupon,
you lost yer left eye,
it's glass noo, colour-
matched and still moves
wi the optic nerve but
deid nonetheless – pupil
doesnae dilate, twitches
not a scintilla. 2K compo
in 1973, that's it, on yer way;
2K compo put doon on you
and ma's first flat in Abbey
-hill. A different type a' justice
wiz employed by your older
brither Harry, a deft boxer,
mair brutish than you, slab-
handed and no so subtle.
Da, you ken ah ken yer
family struggled like nowt
ah've known: social services,
collecting sheep shite off
Arthur Seat for coppers
lifted back off ye, deid sister
afore you met yer teens,
five of you, all scattered. Poul,

yer own Danish faither,
was fierce fires, broth of
bile, a pot boiling ower
at the best o' times, went
blind in his forties, kept yis
crawling roond the council
estates; kept yis, just. Nae
wonner you were so often
warring wi the warl, jumping
doon the throats of shadows.
Aboot that time at Universal
Studios in Florida when I
didnae 'hink to sit oot the 3D
Back to the Future ride
and we laughed kenning
the glasses wouldnae work
on you . . .

Finding Grace
A Love Story: Chapter I

The first time was for the thrill in it;
a secret, sickly joke. He was
popular at college, respected
by the tutors, on for a first in Faust, an
upper second on Fraud; callow yet
adaptable, handsome, not disarmingly
so, but notable when carried well.

He prowled through the bushes in his
burgundy hoody, honed in on a spot
shrouded by trees – autumn's worldly
embrace. A paved path stretched out
and lay down in front of him like an old
man on a park bench. Fifty beaming windows
in full exposure: lampshades winked,

curtains flashed tails, a series of small
lightspills illuminated the walkway. He edged
forward, so on the cusp, toes curling into
the fringes of the path, spine against a conifer,
just-off upright. It was 22.05 and he felt
movement and heat of students in halls:
late-night swotting, lovers snuck-in,

clammy movie-watchers, the smug, sticky,
bored and lonely. He was camouflaged
and motionless for twenty minutes before
final light seeped into soil; he unzipped,
began to caress. Clutching then
tugging, eyes racing from window to
window, breathing through his teeth.

It wasn't until the final moment
he'd steady his vision, home
in on a winner, a wheel of fortune
concluding its spin. He landed in the middle,
third window from the left, a girl in a silver
nightgown, inches from the glass
brushing her hair, wet lips

slightly pursed, eyes daggering the dark.
As it came to a carnal close he was
biting down, salivating, exhaling,
gyrating, the back of his head on
rough bark. Eyelids shut, then open,
a thirsty gaze refocusing detail
definite and clear. She was looking

right at him, warmly and coolly,
as if she could see him, as if she had *always*
seen him. Under night's cape, an earthy
dress, he was surely no more than a

silhouette, smudges, a twitch. This story
had made the *Durham Gazette* a week ago:
'Male, suspicious, spotted outside

St Mary's (all-girls) College,
lurking in the bushes, footprints found.
Ladies beware'. Most had thought it a ruse,
a rouge student penning themselves silly.
He tidied his bits away, slowly, carefully,
as if packing luggage; she continued
to stare, blushed even, faintly smiling,

placed brush on windowsill: a delicate
bow, then closed the curtains. This was a
reciprocated ceremony! This was her,
he knew it now, impetus and purpose,
shimmering Grace. He needed Grace,
as she did him; so must come back
but never again would his eyes parade

the windows – roulette becomes
a game of darts. From the belly of
perversion – up and out from in it – his
Grace: plucky, willing, demure, as if in
a dream, the air around her quiet, all bar
starlight dimmed; some day soon, he
would step out of the shadows and be seen.

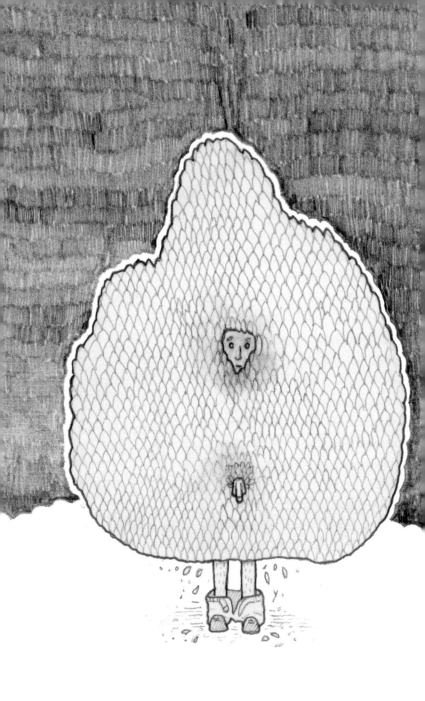

James Dovetail

Guiltlessly you told me, for you, eating
baked beans was tedious. We sat, at eighteen,
undergraduates in the Great Hall of Durham
Castle, ready to split ourselves open. We
learned to drink coffee and wine, I did,
you already knew how. In some ways you
took me the furthest I've been – it was
a darker shade for distance, less earthy, more
peerless black and cosmic risk. Even now, *friend*,
I'm not sure if I loved you then or hated you –
in knowing that, we both were powerful.

Rallying against my gawky thoughts, yours
reigned supreme; to your Mensa I provided
menace, violent bursts of entertainment,
less recondite, more rooster, ponged all
brand new out the box to formal dinners.
This was week one, and I should have got it
as you poked around the plate –
a fussy shopper avoiding beans for breakfast.
I agreed in principle, dismissed half of mine,
scraped the rejected crew into
an overflowing muck bucket. What waste –

I knew I'd let myself down; my heart
sunk with those beans that my dad
took cold with ketchup for supper.
A beany first of a thousand compromises
that led me from seedy after-hours
soirées at Number 10 Downing Street
to letting go of my girlfriend's hand,
to boarding lights, to Las Vegas where, still
high on pills, you told a young Blair you fucked
his dreams just before the air stewards
and birthday cake arrived. Let's wince
to think where this might have ended:

I read you like a clever comic,
you thumbed me like a trashy magazine.

life of owen

reilly, stirrer of porridge;
ranger of rumble and squabble,
brown bauble eyes for which
any kind of terror will do;
my immediate martyr
could find something
to drown for in a pack of
burton's biscuits; raw you were,
riling, hoodwinker, hurter
justified by hurt – this
beautiful hypocrite; try
foraging for fruit old chum:
maybe in the flesh or seeds,
or in the way the juice electrifies
gum and makes a hymn
of taste buds, is a cause
to live with (old chum);
when it comes to you,
any kind of terror will do:
your paw plunged into the fire,
held until the skin seared,
burning sticky, like pudding,
like gum; we're raking leaves
off our faces, sarah and me,

kettles trying to hide
their steam; I capitulate,
yank you out to hysterical victory.

i often wonder how long you
would have toasted, how bloody, how
pus-y – you had a low threshold
for physical pain, like cats
for wet; you have new clothes
i've not seen you out of
and you're never naked
without being seen.

you as a view out a train window
would be busied bees, frogs
holding hands, glass lagoons
and unicorn stars;
not the next apocalypse
or a bludgeoned baby bird, slathered
in blood; despite the way you whistle
and your crooked teeth
you touched me, like me, like
nobody touched me, this is something
for others (all worship-y),
i watched you gaffer tape your soul
back to the bottom
of your shoe, metaphor
melting in my mouth

i would have no need to write this poem
if occasionally
we crossed paths
wide eyed and chatty with an,
ohhhhh you're missing
kisses, missing those
flippered feet we never had
to swim away, me too, with cheeks
still pinchable, *best on my way* –

missing you is not agonizing
or forlorn but like being told
to turn down great music
you're about to turn up.

I'm a PC

Reilly's chest puffs out like
a pair of bibles. Hushed secrets
with sharp edges and sour endings
meet moist September air.

It's 6 a.m., we've slept as stowaways
in an empty venue in Cowgate's
underbelly; now awake, yolking things
together, like why and where exactly;

hollow guts, tangle and chomp. Behind
the bar is barren, the walls sweat
off Fringe posters, wheeze sympathetically.
Last night's memory is flimsy yet stoic,

like tiny knots refusing to come
undone. A eureka moment takes hold
of Reilly: the shows have ended, yes,
but they've left a booking office in their wake

full of prize computers and chintzy accessories
workies have slacked in shipping off. In
tactics unspoken, a flanking trolley is
battlerammed through a thin glass office door,

filled with bounty, greedily as we'd guzzle
free beer. We've time to curtsey, remove
our hats, stare penetratively into defunked
CCTV cameras, frame an invisible legacy.

Two Dell desktops are the prize takings, steel
shelved, covered with a sprawling Mac,
wheeled off as if for surgery. It felt brave
and necessary to a childish cause, we loved

each other. With cargo, flew towards the Meadows,
fizzy as cheap wine for a quick sale;
crazed glints in our narrow eyes, squinting
for flares of morning light.

Invitation for Luncheon with Caddy D

It was lunch at yours at two o'clock,
June 2006. I, fresh back from six months
carousal through seven countries on
a borrowed budget, exploded into
my parent's summer full of vodka, arrogating,
holding the world up tae false charges.
Screaming and bags still packed, it was off
to Owen Morrice's where Owen Reilly
took refuge under my named ticket.
Thing is, that was us both fucked.
So it was heids doon on Porty beach,

the Meadows, Cowgate, an occasional
couch; mobiles volleyed into the sea,
bits of begging, liberating every zooped
-up vessel of white cider we could lay
hands on. It was a fifty-pence payphone
call to a London girlfriend, an egregious
spin on troubles to trigger wire transfers
for hostel money to spend on any'hing
but. It was two twenty. Lunch was at yours
at two o'clock. I deposited Reilly in Nicolson
Square, with the collective spoils.

You'd asked me to pick up a starter –
it was not well received that I hadn't.
On your call, I retrieved Reilly, *on*

your call, willowy and giddy as a
naughty pup I brought him in.
There were other guests: art school
sorts, fashionably dressed and affable
had it not been for us being bomb
builders. Choice contretemps, a quip
or two: they soon cleared oot.
Are you going to be okay, Lorrell

remarked as she made her excuses
not really waiting for your sanction.
You politely called us
into question, usurped our throne
of loose ideals, undressed this faux
homelessness. Alas our machine-gun
mouths and haughty wit
built a wall that couldn't crumble.
An invitation upstairs
to look at your work diffused
the cacophony. It was

a conclusion and an eviction but
not before I marveled at your
photographic achievements –
heartening to see this still necessary.
I could see in your eyes a fondness
for me, it carried sympathy, praise
and expectation; it was, perhaps,
overgenerous. As we collected

our things – summer scarves,
boozy dregs, lighters and pens – you
made some weak remark about us

bettering ourselves and me
getting ma hair cut. The door
closed and re-opened in an instant
to high-pitched hysteria, tears,
dribble, howls of hurt, *give it back*
give it all back, how could you do this?
True befuddlement hits like a thug,
realization follows: Reilly, left unattended,
had rinsed the place! Down
the corridor, I stripped him:
Bob Dylan record, flat's communal

pack of Lucky Strikes, coffee liqueur,
a smidge over seven pounds
in change. These were grudgingly
accepted, acceptance with conniption,
vitriol, a sequel slam of a heavy
door. It transpired you'd brandish
this as a cunning ploy: my gaining
Reilly audience, keeping you entertained
while he filled his pockets. I resent
such accusation, even now – the whole
thing was much sloppier than that.

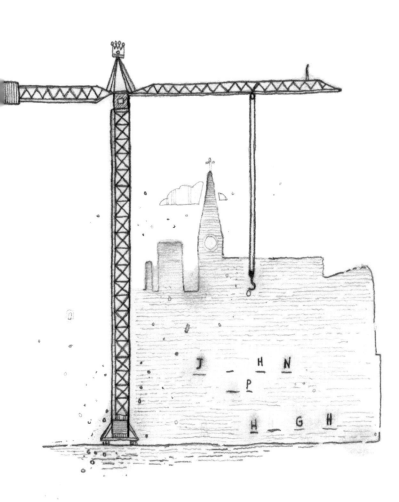

John Up High

One second it was all:
just a gram or two off the ounce
test the product a few films few bottles
natter prattle crackle we're off to London
the morrow rest'll get shifted no bother tell
me about how you get on with your dad and what
about brothers and sisters you got any I've loads right
fucking eh love this film I demand booze too why's he all
morbid 'n' shit that no birds fancy him when he's got drugs and
peev life of Reilly really that's the thing about Manchester trumps
anywhere for easy access to cheap gear dropped-off to the door and
the music man it's just as good as it gets Roses Mondays Joy Division walking
along canals past the old Haçienda and pow wow it's like all over you
as if you fell in the water aye dads are a fucking pain in the arse but you have
to love them that thing between a lad and his old boy it's an emotional
skyscraper; this hotel squat is boss fifty nicks a month each look at the view too
that's real Manchester no Northern Quarter wank bar up its own arse with a
fancy curling straw no boyo nowt but muck works proper boozers pool tables
and darts I like climbing have I ever told you that stay put give us a bit and
answer your phone when I ring ya one more line first though fucking ZAP
batteries charged I'm leaving this station

> [672 seconds of enthused self-philosophy
> and incessant fidgeting later]

can you see me look out the window to the right there a yellow crane
with red trim um up fucking top spectacular this king of the whole
city I can see your shadow at the window geeze and I should know
I'm living in it right two ticks and I'm back with you rack up
another couple of decent ones now we might as well stay up till bus
leaves in a few hours from Chortlon I'm not tired are you well good
we can sink a few swift pints beforehand.

You must have shot up that crane like a maniac:
back by my side less than ten minutes
later. Despite braggart best intentions, I dozed off –
didn't have the gumption see. You were still awake
that time the next day, shaming us all. 300 feet tall
you bragged the mental monster stood. Truth is,
you either never came back down
or you were always that high.

Birthday BBQ, 2008

A hoop of sky, midsummer blue,
clouds as sparse as ducks
on city ponds. Atop my roof garden,
Kentish town, our disparate lot
chewed chicken bones, sunk wine
and beer, picked at all picky bits. Forty
of us, too many, lawyers, dole boys,
swindlers, call-centre operators,
students and bar-staff, all gambol,
gambling on the same birthday
bash. John, you were ragged-
tongued and dangerously toothed:
honesty borne from the same strand

of nakedness that made your friendship
glow. Naveed, you sat patiently
toasting three Halal sausages on your own
disposal barbeque, making jolly
remarks to a pal in advertising. John
greeted you with a 'playful' *alright,*
Paki? then talked about how he loved
Paki food. My sour hiss, John shook
off with a, *nah, my sister's married*
to a Paki, we're great friends –

it's all good. I know for a fact
that brother-in-law slung powder and
chanced his hand. This *one*, Naveed,

Huddersfield born, a Kebab shop
owner's son and Cambridge graduate,
worries about what drunk and drugged
bams rant to his dad while waiting
on their döner meat and chips. John
ambled off, Nav, we laughed past it,
you said, *no worries chuck I've heard
much worse*. Reluctantly my jaw
returned to grinding charred meat
on a soggy bun, but I recall that crappy
plate even now; crappy taste, crappy
crappy flecks, stuck between my teeth.

Manchester John: Episode II

A graduate of zimmer-frame to crutches,
odd to have to meet you on my own,
leaving friends huddled around nonsense
on a TV screen as we stroll to a pub
nearby, order baked tatties: burnt skins

layered up with cheese and onion, washed
away in pints. I told you I was happy to see
you alive, gloried in it; inveighed against
you mostly mocking, canting, relishing
in the cheek of me. We drunk, got

drunk and boasted drunkenly; I had
a ticket home that never got printed.
On your command we met a man,
ominous blackheads peppering his snoz
like poppy seeds cast over light sand;

a pylon growled overhead, his teeth
were crocodile clusters, his son
had just died in a farming accident. I offered
feeble condolence, settled the bill. I could say
you bullied me into it, buying heroin a month

after your second overdose, me, hapless, high
on the zeal of seeing you standing. I could
whistle-blow plenty, blend in dark edges; truth is,
we've been avalanching together
from the moment we met. So, in a park,

opposite the halls of Manchester Met,
we burnt brown, tooted off silver
foil until even the dark sap scorched bare.
There was a moment of torpor, lying
supine on cut grass below birdsong,

the stillest scene in a busied city.
We had not injected this time – that
was something; but like a balloon over-
blown and burst, all warmth inside flooded out.
Gut-wrenching I vomited up

into the moment and down my right side.
Left on the 19:45 from Manchester,
Piccadilly to London Euston, tank empty,
ashamed, tasting raw onion
and cheap orange cheese.

Christmas at Omega Sauna

Clichéd as it comes, and it does come,
the carnal cavalcade, the talent
parade, ladies in procession
as show ponies, eight of them,
perfumes in riot, lined up against
the shooting wall, all colours, all
races, lathered in lingerie, spandex,
garish nursing outfits. Naz,
a City slicker, now a partner
in the firm, knows nowt
of procrastination, picked his
winner before the race began;
in his shadow Rupert zooms off with
febrile pace, hypnotic fervour,
just heard a mumble then *tits*. I'm
there for fifteen minutes like a contestant
on a quiz show, spouting aw sorts
of gibberish till shepherded off
by the bullish maître d'; coupled
with a Thai girl who can 'put her legs
behind her head in two seconds flat'.
Naz's settled the tab so I crack
into the Champagne and cocaine
and offer the same to undressing Kee –
who about slaps me when
I suggest she keeps clothes on.

Kee's from Chiang Mai Province:
we talk of Elephant Camps and spices
at the night market, skinny dipping
in Ping River, water festivals
and border runs to Burma; as if
her bones had softened, she's
laughing at all my touristy
revelations, crap pronunciations;
a few months my junior:
I'm only twenty-two. We slam another few
flutes of bubbles and I snake off
with a wink and a cuddle; noticing her
slip a number in my pocket
but keeping up the façade.

I scale the crippling gradient
of the stairwell, more like a ladder,
up and out and over. Madame yells
behind me: *Will we see you*
on Christmas Day – special prices
for our well-behaved customers?
Free candy cane with every girl.
Sexy festive outfits! is the last
snatch before her market pitch
cascades out of earshot.
The other two are already out,
at the rendezvous in the Oxford.

Over the road with pub oak
I order Chang lager and wipe snow
off my boots. Festiveness blares
out of speakers and mouths, bleeds
brilliantly into total light. *You smash*
her then? Naz growls, lip
quivering; even his breath is lascivious.
A smile, skewwhiff, sinks and flops
down the side of the sofa;
I think what to say. Merry rhythms
drive along my jaw, *naw mate*
just talked about Thailand. His wry
smile caves in and out comes
the rapturous, *course you fucking did*,
winking towards the rafters,
a balloon of hot air.

WI
Bréon George Rydell back in Eduardo's Place

*Scottish National Gallery of Modern Art, Edinburgh
where Sir Eduardo Paolozzi's Studio has been re-homed.*

Ahhhh, *this* fragmented civilization, this
hunk of Chelsea hoisted out
the ground and laid out like a six
course dinner – yourself a man starved.
This is Paolozzi's studio, in Dean Village,
its myriad everything saw a young Rydell
from boyhood tae manhood, hours melting
as ice in sun. Get that ear in close,
hear him rumble through spoils
and spills, offer a paw, offer plaster
wrapped in newspaper like hot chips on
winter solstice, passed with a knowing nod,
a wet lipped whistle: *Inspiration*. In-
spiration, cargo loaded in deep pockets
or bound inside a leather satchel.
It was. is. all. still. here: models,
tools, toys, saws, hammers, wood
propellers, his *almost* architecture;
packs of books, wolf-feral, each
limb sculpted, lissome, twisted,
an octopus reaching any which way.

Paolozzi presents the head dissected, his
Vulcan keeping sentry as we pay
vigil to a memory. From behind the gaudy
red rail you floated up, off
the polished floors of the National
Galleries, haloing the room, bouncing
one last time on the studio bed
then exiting in a grand finale via the highest
window: life pouring out where light
slides in. We regrouped outside, I pulled
you down by your gingham socks
and off we went for tapas as if
going about the dailies. *Goodbye*

Eduardo, you toasted,
gnawing tiger prawns, fingers
laced in parmesan.

Wı(III)

Bréon, yes Bréon from
before, Bréon who talked in
dreams beyond fuller dinner plates,
superior wine and less hours in
an office. Bréon whose electric finger-
-tips could zap geese, who during
tectonic eruptions reverse-wormed
off the mattress; whose eyes
couldn't watch the telly. From
stories of Scottish fisherman,
their sadness and scathing traits –
this same Caledonia of mine – to
the Hollywood Hills and Dream Tower
Inn; an austere familial code but really
there's no blood in relation and
that's simply wonderful. Current-of
-night Bréon (all the divine
complications of faith) who said,
don't label me, as I put my shoes
back on, *welcome to the family*, and,
no judgment here; so I showed him
scales, purpled veins; splurged,
let a pickled liver plop into play. Bréon
who sat in a hospital bed crippled
and nattered with a crook, offering
one totem: *either you're real, it's*

real or it's not. I sort of got it then –
swore to it. Bréon who made me feel
girlish and silly, so much so I began
lusting to be a planet again; *decommissioned*
Pluto stop sulking, be a planet again:
orbit uncountable stars, loosen your axis,
be part of a solar gang. A planet,
yes a planet, and the same Bréon
who was wind once that ran like
soft ribbon over my stinging cheek
on a spring morning in Kentish Town, then
came back and knocked me off my feet
for kicks; who was sun once, rising
when it seemed impossible, then burning
my skin when I fell asleep drunk, but
who is most like moon: gloaming,
a lunar lullaby, like a brother,
a lover, carouseling, pirouetting,
an interstellar pilot, never knowing
if he's due to land or how much
of the flight I'll see. Bréon, moon
for me, felt most from behind thick
fog when thought lost, *it's exactly there*
I'd say: its pull of gravity, its maniac
brightness, howl now, *I am moon too,*
do not switch me off
like a night-light. As if to blink
back the ink-black turns
plum, shifts navy.

When Carla Moved Out

Without you I have no butter,
no shampoo, no part of me
that you make happen, empty
shelves, cupboards bare, a soup
of snot for breakfast, a bowling
ball belly. I am glad you took
the silk pillowcase I bought you
from John Lewis. I am sad you left
flamingo slippers I ordered online
– I had to chuck them out.
Their feathers thinned, I grew
tired of sniffing them, my feet
were too bulky. When you moved
out I found another corner
of the room had got
too big for its boots, I stopped smelling
of rain and red playdough.

Hey Ho Here Comes Colin

(for Colin Jarvie 1962–2012)

To unleash a show, we voyaged to outside Ayr
on cup final day, the Robert Burns Birthplace
Museum, to be exact. I didn't know you
were coming, didn't know what you were
to know. It was an intimate audience – staff,
a few curious visitors, a lost passerby
and Colin Jarvie, Napoleon solo, all the way from
Edinburgh. Fastidiously styled (as ever, I learned):
charcoal flattop, baby blue scarf with amber
shimmer, a fitted tweed three piece – ochre jacket,
matching trousers, waistcoat of dark emerald;
a sharp patterned tie, that and all the big

breezy smiles puckered lips could muster.
By the journey back we were cads and
cadre, a low slung sun across the train table.
We talked about old bands that blew your
socks off, wild happenings at Club Taboo,
being the only black boy at Clerie High; loving
London. Leaving London, all the colours you
saw in those Acapulco busses, the ubiquity of
Coke-a-Cola swirls in South America;

not-at-all being interested in the scores
coming in; the certainty with which things
seemingly infallible can collapse,

Edinburgh bravado. You were a collector,
I got that straight away: lenses, people,
people through lenses; populariser of Polaroid
film, harvester of plaudits, some knowingly,
worn with goofy pride – *I'm Davy Henderson's
favourite flavor of yogurt* – drunk and silly
with it. Others surfaced posthumously: The Colin
Jarvie Photography Award, broke in by London
College of Printing; that and everything
we said about you at Summerhall, in praise of
shadows, in place of only having itched it.
Telling dear and close ones, telling them

over and over, *he would have bloody loved
this*. A remark as rickety and recyclable as
brimful of ritualistic comfort, like tea offered
to a weary traveller. Your Polaroid SX-70 sits
on my office shelf, the note reads, *One of Colin's
first cameras, it doesn't work, it won't shut, it
carries only ornamental value. I thought you'd
like it*. Despite the caveat, I sent it off
to Cameratiks to be repaired – a new
something to do with a shutter plus geeky
nurture. £56.15 all in. Not an insignificant
sum; not much either, considering.

Transmorphisizing

One day a carpenter turned into
Chester Drawers. It happened in an
orderly fashion, from head to toe:
the scaffold, set in fragments, cast
a body into structure around him.
The top drawer was his head, a swamp
of photograph albums and sketchbooks,
torn, part complete, moist so as some
of the inks had run. The middle drawer
was his heart – it had fallen off the runners,
jammed so tightly that to open it would
split the delicate wood; it would remain
closed, widowed. The bottom drawer
was his gut and groin combined, gut *and*
groin, full of undigested red meat,
the booming sound of laughter. A long
bratwurst sausage jerked and spasmed
on a plate, it was his sexual inadequacy.
The base of the frame was his feet, steadfast
despite boils and blisters becoming chips
and chinks, although never really moving
anywhere of great importance. Whilst being
perfectly vertical takes slight courage,
he felt wood a hollow offering in place
of fleshy sacrifice and what sort of flimsy
faith would honour that with gifts or
peace. If this *was* him dying, he'd have

rather been a rhinoceros running
rampage on a French township – he'd
read about such metamorphosis
in the Theatre of the Absurd: brutal
and beastly, one last lunge at
something memorable and strong.
His was a feckless arsenal, ability to
creak and stiffen; brief firewood, he
could rot, though the wood was once
much more alive; his greatest feat,
something most human, hinges
that could come undone.

Greetin' fur Gretna Green

Ach, Gretna Green I'm sorry, pal,
I really did mean tae visit, really did
want tae, instead I'm writing this
fae Indonesia, Ubud, beside a lover,
in and out of napping, last night's
daffy squabble ripening on our lips;
but breakfast beckons and we'll wash
it aw away with miso soup
and watermelon juice. She's lovely,
the lover, hus stories of yer service
stations (aye, I asked), firing up
the A74, broke the border many times
wi her faither barkin boldly.
A caveat: there is no runaway
bride here, no blacksmith's anvil,
no Jane Austin adaptation, no any
of those most-talked-about traits
yer likely sick to death of hearing.
It's yer starling murmurations
that draw the most fae me, them
reminders that sometimes 'hings
spin so fast it looks as if they're still, them
amorphous blobs of a thousand lives
shape-shifting with inky synchronicity
– them like baubles on yer pylons, them
I'm guessing, hoping, dress yer postcards.

But that's the noo and I've hud months
to dress myself in you and of the months
before ma excuse is just as weak. While
others would huv sought you oot, extolled
yer charms, got manky in yer dirt,
shared wedding tales where life wi you
was a glass brimfu', I the fud, did not.
So I'm sorry to your broken-hearted,
I'm sure we'd get along, savour breaths,
break bread, slam shots thigither
at the disco, neither o' us dancing.
Fecklessly, for you, I imagine aw these
pusses on the streets, the good folks
of Gretna Green: trendy jackets,
umbrellas splitting in savage wind,
tired faces, smiles, fancy hats
– but then this is how I see
us most, in shifting winds, yer twigs
breaking under feet that urnae
mine. So let's get to it, this is
what I've got tae give – you've muscled
yer way into many mighty moments
here, mighty as I've kent – ornate
carvings of Hindu Goddesses
on stone temples peppered
wi you, elephant towel art wi you
in their een, my sunburn stinging, you
part of pulse; you climbed wi me and lover

to the top of Tegenungan Waterfall,
clambered into sheets without a fold
and as I unwrap lover's legs
fur a flash, ye dirty bugger, my mind drifts
into you. If we are whit we are
because of whit we're no,
me and you, we're forged a little
closer than I ever would huv thought,
than places cherished and desired,
your platitudes of the still-to-be-imagined
in ma takeoffs and landings, up here in
the stratosphere, you; in Ubud, caked
in sweat, you, clinging ever tighter.
So perhaps I'll see you after,
perhaps to share a photo, in which
we'll, both of us, look eager
to be ignored. On the plane
above the clouds, the view belongs
tae masses of folks but is at the same
time entirely mine *until*, yes,
ma mind drifts back to you, Gretna
Green, to the poem unwritten,
the promise never kept.

Humping Cows

A response to a text stating: 'Dear Michael, My commute to work was made a little tricky by cows trying to hump across my path. That is all. Hollie X'

Dear Hollie,
Let them hump.
Go on, let them, cheer 'em on,
applaud 'em on finishing –
could be that randy bovine
breed, could be that warm
weather, something in the water,
a shag long overdue, perhaps
the sweet perfume of sex
fizzing in the air has set
their olfactory senses
ablaze and they need just
a little taste tae cool doon, a lick
of the icy lollie to offset
the loin's inferno – hear hear
tae a carnal anecdote, hear
hear to humping till aw light
vanishes, and the sun sleeps,
and the moon bullies through the sky.
It could be that . . . could be
even supporting a Koo's
copulation seems part of

a spirited free-thinking move
towards righteousness, beatitude,
tender songs. But I'm no fur fooling
nae one, I'm love-struck and horny.

FUCK!

Text: I spent two years just having sex,
Michael; a lot of sex.

FUCK!

I sent you a poem by Kim Addonizio
on having terrible sex: *You look fatter*
with your clothes off, the twat
inaugurates, summoning Kim atop,
indolent as a toff beckoning his setter
to a rigged hunt; the second command: to
face away, thataway. Insulted, resentful,
unenthused but it carries on, Kim
slides up on thighs and down on dick,
prepped to be fucked staring at a stain
on a wall that *resembled Florida,*
blessed now, not to be eyeballed, to have
a mind meandering avenues away from
what was going on down there,
his cock *like a speculum* as he
groaned. A fucking speculum!

FUCK!

I knew you'd reference right back, draw
upon it, seed yourself quite brilliantly,
into its dank pit, weed things (like men and
moments) out, toss your residue into
the same soggy compost heap, to
disintegrate, fetidly, fester before
brewing into nourishment.
You did, sure you did, and rightly so:

> *Text: God I hate that sort of sex. Awful.*
> *Tragic. Easy to be pulled into; no more.*

FUCK!

I feel cowed by your openness,
like taking a first drag of a strong cigarette
amongst prodigious smokers, level
pegged from the outset, eased-in
by generous presumption. But here at this
metaphorical party, all together (me, you, and
your sexual experiences), I'm my meeker
self, laughing too hard, then sullen,
eyes over attentive, so 'not with
the programme'. Before long I'm
furtively slipping out the kitchen
window, sliding down the fire-escape;
unannounced, of course, and blushing.
All to get blind drunk, alone,

in a dive bar, to piss in the gutter
because the queue for the toilet
was too big and garrulous and full
of 'getting to know one anothers' and eaves-
dropping. The gaggle at the party
aren't messing about, some
might sympathise but there's no time
on the clock for that, so they all
just fuck each other again and again
 – nobody gets sore or tired
because each ameliorates the next
pasting themselves creamily back
together, reinforced and randy.

Hours later, I howl up at the window
– lights are on, sexy chitchat abseils
down, fireworks fly from the bedrooms;
I ring the buzzer, I've changed my
mind, ring the buzzer; ring
the buzzer.

A Year, Aye?

It's been a year, I'm not mistaken,
a year, so nope not dalliance or tryst,
no *whit a whirl that wis, put oan*
the telly, see whit's we've missed.
Ma heart flutters, no letting go,
ma organs inside chatter, puffed
and full in parley. *It's quite absurd*
the lungs might craw, *his breathing*
never steadies; third flock of
butterflies this week we've netted.
Belly bubbles readied; another strange
and cawing noise the throat lets loose –
it's really getting quite obtuse;
in somersault with each trapeze
the stomach hosts . . . is this really
happening chaps? Yup and yes,
here comes the post. A year unfurled
wi'oot confetti, a whizz pop where
did that come from and go to?
A year and no idea whether any closer
but clear as Spanish summer days:
I couldn't utter ultimatums even if
I meant 'em. Positive and petrified,
positively petrified, but, yup and yes,
if you'll huv it, unlike the wine
stain on yer blouse, my mess is
here to stay.

Totem Pole Capable

Who's the fucking big man now eh? Who's the big man!

There he is on top of the bonnet of a car, palms upturned,

arms spearing out, caught cruciform, showing signs

of disillusionment, volatile, strident. A moment past

he's clambered the scrap metal giraffe sculpture outside

the busy Omni Centre, fastened onto its back like a buckle,

looped around its sturdy neck, declared himself

a cowboy, steam billowing from pistol, fingers

ablaze, pores teary with whisky. Dismounted only

to antagonize a ten body, tall, well-flexed gaggle of

a stag-party – you would describe them as 'of rugby build',

totem pole capable, physically equipped; myself as

milky and wispy, unsteady on the feet. I'm told

a humorous twist changed the tempo, something stark

and bare, lunar, led me on my way, undeservedly

unscathed. Remember now being in a nightclub, we don't go

to nightclubs, I'd been on spirits, it's best we stay away

from those, neon too. From one car on to the next,

a sort of plié as the ritual ends. At least it's capturing

the madness, so that someone much smarter might

take the time to work it all out. Then again, why the

fuck would they bother?! Now bolt upright in an empty bed,

I see a phone blinking. We must discuss these matters at once.

Conversation Overheard in Craigmillar
Dental Practice

*I quietly wait my turn in the busy waiting room. It's packed
to the rafters with mas, das, cads, bairns & dugs; toys
tapping, TV barking.*

Aye, they let anyone in eh?

Ruining this bewtiful country.

See I never felt I wis a racist, just pointing oot the
blinking obvious – things that adabody cun see, but noo,
noo I do – cause they're rubbing this 'whit's right and whit's
wrong' pish aw ower our pusses.

*Ken. They call us white trash and Scottish scum and all that shite
and whit happens . . . sweet fuck all. But when I call them oot,
some fuckin do-gooder threatens to call the Joe Rolis fur 'so-called'
racism.*

Bullshit eh?

*Everybody hates them being here, it's just most dinnae ken what to
do aboot it. They're taking aw the hooses and stinking them oot wi
curry and banana breid whilst hunners of Scots are oan the street.*

It's no racist to hoose our ain first or to ask some of them to leave so as Scottish-born folks can get into the gaffs. They'd huv you think you were sending them off to the electric chair rather than back to their ain fuckin country.

I'll bet ya anything most of them probably fought against us in the war, eh! And another thing, ma pal Liam McClay fae Magadeline got kicked oot his digs the other day to make way for a foreign family. There's mair of them I suppose but he's one of oors!

Just shows yi, I went to primary school with Liam. Sound wee laddie. Funny as fuck – would wind the teachers right up.

Still on the old scag likes?

Aye. But he's no harming anyone but himself is he?!

Course he's no. It's his country and his boady he cin do whit he wants wi it. It's no as if he's looking after anyone's bairns is it?

Ken Gail McGraw fae Bingham? Well she was telling it straight on the bus the other day, driving past them new hooses in Piershill – 'get them funny colours oot' she said 'there's no enuf room fur them'.

Well . . . did it no just aw kick off. Did it NO!

Aye? Whit happened likes?

*Did the driver no just come up and chucked her aff – aye, he did.
She'd paid her fare and everything. He said there's CCTV on here
and passengers might find that sort of talk offensive. Said he didnae
per say, but if he was seen to do nuthin aboot a 'racist incident' then
he could lose his job. Jesus fuck – imagine that!*

Craaaaaaaazy likes. It's – how do you put it – unjustice!?

Fucking right it is.

*Now I was thinking, eh – and hopefully you agree wi me – I'd
rather be robbed off a Scot than yin o' them any day. Cause
although it's a shiter, at least that wiy you know there's a chance of
one of oor folks benefitting; and it's definitely not going taewards
any of them terrorist plots.*

Makes sense like.

I'm Jean by the way.

Nancy.

[A voice from the distance]: Jean Dewar. Calling Jean
Dewar.

R v Brown

*R v Brown [1994] is a House of Lords judgment in which
a group of men were convicted for their involvement in
consensual sadomasochistic sexual acts over a ten year period.
They were convicted of 'unlawful and malicious wounding'
and 'assault occasioning actual bodily harm' contrary to
sections 20 and 47 of the Offences against the Person Act 1861.
The key issue facing the Court was whether consent was a
valid defence to assault in these circumstances, to which the
Court answered in the negative.*

it's ma boady
MA BOADY
MA baws tae nail to table
ma table to huv baws nailed tae'em
so dinnae tell me naw when
I cin tattoo ma puss wi umpteen spider's webs
or go ten roonds wi big Kenny Anderson,
throat fuck fifteen inch jaggy dildos,
skull as much absinthe as ah fancy
wi fags hanging oot my eyes and ears;
I cin snort Vindaloo powder tae celebrate
ma hundredth piercing or fling maself
aff the top diving board ut the Commy Pool
(wi nae chance o' a graceful landing);
so take yer section
20 and yer fucking 47 and yer offensive

risk tae family life and yer harmful tae boady and mind
and yer labels of cultish violence and shove it right
up the tightest cavity in sight!
If pleasure derived fae infliction of pain
is such an EVIL 'hing then tell
aw them suckers getting mirried
wi faith in love and fidelity and aw that pish
that they're in fur a rough
ride and a long stretch
in their nearest HMP
'cause that's the stuff
that's the STUFF
that really stings.

Free Personality Test, Sir?!

Administered by the Church of Scientology,
– only one of its kind? Our measurable
results with post-test consultation
translate IQ, choices, and aptitudes
into future success and happiness;
your potential is waiting for you
– seek yourself out.

Ach go on then, I heard myself
mutter (a little incredulous); see
it was pishing doon, I hud no
brolly; my feet, wild wet.

Are you composed sir? The lassie says.
Aye, ah goes. *Then let's begin.*
Let's get to the bottom of you.

Without a whistle or a blink
I blurt it out, uneasy, angsty
in manic pace, from salted lips: *I am*
a reckless sort who's hurt many
good people – I've mitigating
circumstances to call upon, choice
caveats, skillfully spun, yet insufficient

for the full acquittal – Lord Buddha.
That said, I do weep at Undercover Boss
(USA), then think to call my parents
back. I drink too much, experiment
with narcotics, get publicly horny;
fictionalise the deaths of close
friends and relatives, the caprices,
eruptions, the violence that follows;
but when real death has wrapped
his spiny fingers around my wrist
I've suffocated several terrible out-
-bursts, fortified myself and those within
grasp. I've lied about simple sugaries,
dressed fripperies in hyperbolic
sheep's wool coats (wolves inside),
then pulled sharp steel truths from
deep within stones, when really, they
could have stayed trapped forever.
I've . . .

The lassie stopped us there likes;
gestured to her computer screen
blinking, uttered, *it's an electronic test.*
In fact sir, I think it's best you go.
So ah did. But fuck me,
had it no just stopped raining,
turned out a beautiful day.

Superstition & Superheroes

The child years of eight to twenty-
  three, I believed in two types of
    power, namely those applicable to me.

    Power one: invisible beams shot
      across city roads by stepping on
        stopcocks and manhole covers.

      When activated, these spray out
        elixir illuminations coating
          passing cars in life-saving light,

          each stomp worth one hit, each
            hit preventing a near-future
              crash – some likely minor scuffles,

            surface scrapes or chinks, others
              the more serious ilk: mangled
                metal, ghoulish wails then wakes.

              Power two is two parted, not
                quite as black and white – an
                  indicator of virtue, not a power

per se. First part is levitation,
focusing then rising, lightening
then loosening, higher I got

the better I'd been going. Second
shake, chameleon traits, the more
good deeds done more supreme

the blue became in the iris
of my een: pigmentation and light,
a fifteen gene association with colour

playing second fiddle to bright
eyed venerability; framing noble
futures. Though my irises

have stayed true blue and I still
float up and out of here, so these
oaths must be hogwash, however

hotly sworn; I've not purposely
stood on stopcocks for years,
have witnessed

countless ghastly accidents,
some scrapes, most the brutal
type, write-offs, fatalities,

though not on tarmac roads
but by fragmentation in people,
of soul and psyche and skin and sure

as all those times as a child,

I could have stopped the clock
if I'd had my wits about me,
instead of admiring

the glints in their eyes.

(In between) Mud & Stars

Through an open window
of a wooden lodge, I watched
a dragonfly prang into a spider's
radials – in a blink the deft
pilot found peril, met harm. Its red
body shimmered, hinted blue, twirled,
wings paddled *and slapped against
the silken glue. Och, stay still,* I thought
*be tactical about this, you're a big
bugger of a beastie compared to those
infinitesimal ropes slung around
you; and right glam – naebody wants
this to end in your demise.*

It was too late, the perfect
little wings had stopped twitching,
became stained-glass miniatures
stilled in light. And so entered
the spider, eight foreboding legs
like dark mascaraed eyelashes,
curled, crooked question marks,
slicing then biting to a kill.

Was this a battle of good
and evil, colours shook out
from heaven versus portentous black;

brink of breakfast or a bloody
murder scene? Like thoughts that
come only with drink, vilely, I knew
it: even more so than the spider, I
was possessor of Herculean strength
– the *only* party that could have switched
the endings. It's like with love, transfixed
you can watch something beautiful
die, hoping umpteen valid
reasons for it will soon surface.

Portree's Lost & Found

Snap! U'm related tae Sorley MacLean:
glugs a Guinness in a oner then recoils
like a proud feline to lick its coat
more golden wi each lap. *No time fur*
poetry in Portree noo, mind, I'm the man
you call aboot lost anchors. Like

an anchor dealer? But no, not
an anchor dealer, more a black
-book scoundrel, off-radar then in deep.
See, sometimes the undercurrents
and fish bite gnarly through the rope
and a ship's anchor leaps free,

spirals, kamikaze, seabed south.
Feckin' Harbour authority'll charge
ye an arm 'n' a leg, two days drinkin'
and plate o' crab ti fetch it – officially!
Unofficially, see me doon Tongdale,
Pier Hotel or Isle Inn. I've a boat,

floats, motor and suit, beer in ma
belly, aye, but the chaos o' them bills
keeps us gallus. I'll get yer auld anchor
back provided I get back wi it. A gully
and gut fu' o' pints later he's
snoozing on the table, laid out

like a string puppet for woodchip.
John MacLean Bryden and I
chortle some but conscience boaks:
the lady behind the bar reminds us
even in yer smawest toons
rain faws different under every cloud.

Calm it is in season, whipping up skirts
and speckling the walkways; but this
is wild unforgiving ocean,
hissin 'n' thrashin
at the land, toying wi this harbour.
My response is nervous: transparent

chuckles buoyed by floats, a line
cast, tongue tae hook – a ghost
lingers above us in the room. I reconsider
and place a half Guinness on the table
for when he stirs. As if in applause
the old bell tolls above the door

and a platter of iced oysters parades past,
glimmering trophy-bright, to a table
of squawking onlookers. With the bell
quiet and table busy, a head cocks
through a window ajar: *yin fur you*,
a sharp tongue spits

like flame to rouse our skipper. *Richt
laddies, back in a jiffy*; sinks the
offering and croaks centred as nitrogen
in chemistry class – *I'll tak the other
half off yis on return*. Through the window
each wave is a swell of laughter

full of froth; skipper changes, slips
one skin off, the next on, a glint
in his gaze says he'd like to stop time:
himself anchorless and free but not
likely to roam anywhere for longer
than it takes for stout to warm.

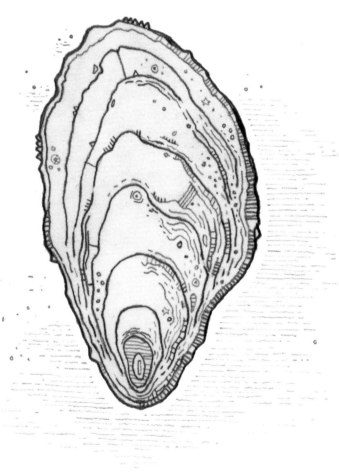

Guide to Space Proofing your Robot Heart

With an aim to travel millions of
miles, still operate by beat, be
sensitive to spry breeze – be mindful,
a hundred mile an hour wind
on Mars is barely felt
what it comes down to is heat,
a lick on the fingertip, how fast
does it cool, your blood. Wind
affects landing and landing is key
but that's getting ahead
of ourselves, you're not off
yet. To get a robot heart cleared
for space you'll have to prove
it is not going to break, Mars
is a bumpy ride, a whirlwind
of milkshake spins. A robot heart
does not have lasers, cannot
cosmic blast bothersome bolides,
can very well smash to smithereens
(*you know that feeling?*).

A champion robot heart
will be made out of recyclables,
busted fragments put back
together know not to break
again. Practise not having your heart

break whenever you can,
connect with all that vibrates,
get stirred and shaken up,
rally against the vacuum of space,
ask yourself are you the right
stuff – material that won't melt
nor come apart at the seams?
They'll want to see your wirings,
see you survive a little damage,
go radish-red from radiation
or cry a sunburnt lament.

Have you considered planetary
protection? You should. Space
must remain contamination free
from your life-forms,
your onion gook and old
rhubarb; bones, teeth,
lockets of hair, juicy knickers:
it is unlikely these things
you keep will thrive on Mars
– have they thus far? No!
So they'll perish just dandily
Sickness, however, is tricky.
Everything must be sterilized:
fish kisses, widowed wishes,
all jewelry given or taken,
the bling-ness in bright eyes.

Being baked at one hundred
and twenty-five degrees
Celsius kills all your darling
bugs, but that's not enough:
there's deadness and ghosts
all over you – wasps behind
curtains, stowaway mites
and who knows what's hidden
in the gooey filling? It is unlikely
you were assembled in a clean
environment, unlikely your
robot heart knows anything
of the 54.6 million kilometer
journey to Mars.

Your robot heart may land
in the type of sea that swallows
ships and scares off krakens
– there are no (reliable) weather
reports available for Mars.
Landing *is* key but an earthly
practice: twist Rubik's
cubes, thread needles, throw
darts to make a bullseye,
slide drawers on runners,
assemble furniture – you'll be
fine, you are an astro-juggler
whose balls jettison a heat

shield, deploy a parachute,
inflate an air bag; be a ball
with bounce, be a ball with
breath, unfold your fuzzy
limbs, feel the earth swell.

In the limelight of your
robot heart is a kit bag.
Check it, it should contain:
an engine, armour, a fist,
an oil painting of a red
plump heart kissed by cold
robot lips; although no
cage is visible, it is likely
there: bend the bars.

Your mission proposal
will take ten to fifteen
years to advance. You
have very little time left.

Deep, deep down

is a motion and a yolk,
is a gluttony, a sweet
soup, my neck tight
and craned; is your open
thighs' honeyed wetland,
summer rain, puddling
now rivering towards
my begging tongue – *shhhhhh*
she's unhooked herself;
so under covers
is a purring, a hushed
zoom, is singing carols,
is blood quickening,
is yelling like riding
rollercoasters, cheeks
full strawberry flush,
is . . . *shhhhhhhhh* . . . is
shhhhhhhhh; deep,
deep down.

Hello, I am Scotland

Who wakes every morning
in a brilliant mood as auburn bursts
cast filigree nets over foreheads
and swingparks and paint themselves
on pavements. Up gets the brickworks,
frost needles arms, winds shriek
through my Munros, gossiping
as another small dug sinks
into deep snow; and the day floats down
like a feather from the sky. *Ach,*
barks a father's voice caught
in the breeze, *let him sing his*
song and paint whitever it is
he cares tae paint. I've a soft spot fur daft
romantics and who wouldnae
grasp fur it, when it really could be it.

My cities breathe in the rivers,
salute the environmentalists: snail
savers, wall walkers, ally
of Elm and Ash. Every day my oceans
swallow five hundred thousand footprints,
strangle gulls in fitted laughter,
emit the salty corpse; seasplash
spears a drunken busker
mixing up his cluster chords.

I, too, forget such simple things,
perhaps have never known
all the numbers of the buses
and their routes, the vagaries in roadworks;
but I *do* remember bonfires
in aw them bellies as whole families
politicised breakfast over toasted soldiers
and eggs unfit and fit for dipping.

We jumped without parachutes,
so they'd have you think (skirted
around each other's glances
like window cleaners avoiding
a high-up mucky splodge); it wasn't that
at all, more a faith in flying.

ACKNOWLEDGEMENTS

Some of these poems have been published in magazines and anthologies: *The Dark Horse*; *Sogo*; *Cold Lips*; *The Café Review*; *Hero*; *Neu! Reekie! #UntitledOne* (Polygon); *Neu! Reekie! #UntitledTwo* (Polygon); *Inspired by Independence* (Word Power Books); *Shelter Scotland: A Christmas Songbook*.

Most of the poems here appear for the first time. Many were written on two residencies: yin at Cove Park and the other in Grez-sur-Loing – on the Robert Louis Stevenson Fellowship. Mighty thanks for these opportunities, Cove Park, Robert Louis Stevenson Trust, Scottish Book Trust and Creative Scotland – ah gret a little with delight being there. Also hat tipped to Maggie, The MacLean family for lending me the keys to Portree (all powers Sorley).

Thanks tae: all the chums, cadre and cads that let me feast on their bizarre lives – yer bobby-dazzlers, in the most part. Especially these ones: Big Gerry Cambridge – fur tirelessly educating this wayward mind, and the blanket of friendship you chucked around us; to Ma and Da – who've kept my heid above water, this ship afloat despite my best efforts to the contrary; Wee Jessie, mon yersel, Grandma (just that); to W1, KWD, CJE and GiGi – for the magics you weave; yes, Hollie McNish – who is every bit as brilliant as these poems shout about – (the mere), I marvel at ye; to Robbie McKillop – for thinking we can make a film together, then setting about making that a reality; tae No.1 The Grange – fur the oyster platter slurped down with gusto; Reilly and John, aye; to those that help make Neu! Reekie! fly (esp Kevin and Kat); to aw the Polygon team – who championed this book before I knew what on earth it was; and to Scott Hutchison for furnishing these pages with your lustrous strokes and curious mind.

Here's to being a bunch of soppy souls thigether – now and forever.

A NOTE ON THE TYPE

Oyster is set in Verdigris MVB – a typeface designed by Mark van Bronkhorst. It is a Garalde text family for the digital age and is inspired by work of sixteenth-century punchcutters Robert Granjon, Hendrik van den Keere and Pierre Haultin.

FREE AUDIO

There are eleven free audio poems that come with this book; email Oyster@PolygonBooks.co.uk to get your free download.